Risk, Resilience, *and* *Redemption*

Published by Tree of Life Books
102 Sandy Ridge-Mt Airy Road
Stockton, NJ 08559

www.treeoflifetreeofjoy.com

Editor/Publisher: Joy E. Stocke
Illustrations and Design: Tim Ogline / Ogline Design

ISBN #979-8-9986981-3-2 (Trade Paperback)

10 9 8 7 6 5 4 3 2

Printed in the United States of America

Risk, Resilience, and Redemption

A MIRACULOUS HOLOCAUST SURVIVAL STORY

FRANK W. BAKER

Tree
of Life
Books

"*I think I'm a fairly happy guy, and I am a grateful guy. I live in the best country in the world, the U.S.A., with the best wife in the world, Bluma. But I carry inside me a very unpretty past, and I worry that…what I experienced in my past others should not experience in their future. Let us all appreciate the freedom we have and guard it and preserve it at all costs.*"

– FELIX GOLDBERG

Bluma and Felix Goldberg,
shortly after their marriage

"As you are probably aware, to review these events in my life is very painful for me. I bear this pain willingly if and only if you the student take into your heart or your experience to so that somehow you and I will have contributed together to diminish the possibility of it ever happening again to any people from any people."

– BLUMA TISHGARTEN GOLDBERG

"As difficult as it is to digest, we need to learn everything we can about the Holocaust. We need to understand that such (an) atrocity happened in one of the most advanced, cultured societies at the time. We need to see what led up to it, how propaganda and prejudice fueled it, how people allowed it to happen. We need to know what hatred can lead to—not just on an individual level, but on a mass scale."

– Annie Reneau, author, quoted on the website,

Upworthy, "Panoramic 'Tour' of Auschwitz."

C O N T E N T S

A NOTE TO THE READER

*T*HE story you are about to read is true. Events have been fact-checked and verified via videotape testimonies as well as through surviving historical documents.

Before we begin, here are a few questions:

What do you know about "the Holocaust"?

Where did you learn about the Holocaust?

Do you know why the Nazis considered Jews to be "an inferior race"?

Do you know that antisemitism led to the Holocaust?

There are so many questions to ask and so many ways for you to find the answers. This book will provide you with some answers.

You may already be aware that there are people who say the Holocaust never happened. They use social media to spread false and malicious information. It is critically important that you question what you read. Don't believe what your read and hear just because it's on the Internet. Look for the truth. It's there in the stories of Jewish mothers, fathers, and children no different from your own parents and siblings, except that they were taken from their homes and forced into ghettos and concentration camps. Six million people did not return, but some did; just ask Bluma and Felix Goldberg.

This is a true story about two people who survived the Holocaust. Bluma Tishgarten and Felix Goldberg were young Polish Jews caught up in the rise of Antisemitism and Adolf Hitler's rise to power. This and other events led to the *Shoah*, the Hebrew word for the Holocaust.

Even though World War II and The Holocaust occurred many years ago, atrocities, genocide, intolerance, prejudice and antisemitism still exist today. The phrase "never forget" was coined as a reminder to remember and to study the past.

– Frank W. Baker
Columbia, South Carolina

HOW IT STARTED

PRESENT DAY AND A LOOK BACK

*I*N January, the Goldberg family visits the cemetery where their parents are buried. Before departing Esther, the youngest, puts her hands on the Mezuzah, (a Jewish ornament whose prayer blesses all who enter and depart a home), and brings her hand to her mouth—a way of showing respect and remembering God.

"Are you OK?" her brother, Karl asks.

"No," she replies.

Henry, the oldest, looks at her kindly, and says, "I understand."

They get into the car for the long ride. They pass The Tile Center in Columbia, South Carolina; the business their late father ran with their mother, Bluma. Felix started the company when they emigrated to Columbia after the war.

At the cemetery, as they walk through headstones toward their parents' graves, Esther, Karl and Henry search the ground for small rocks before they reach their parent's headstone. In a ritual of respect, practiced since biblical times, each of them quietly puts a rock on top of the headstone. They are contemplative. Esther pulls out a tissue from her purse and begins to dab her eyes. She looks up and says: "Do you want to say it?"

Karl responds with a nod in the positive.

He pulls out of his pocket a small piece of paper with some writing on it: it is the Kaddish—a traditional Jewish prayer recited in memory and honor of those who have passed away. Before departing, Henry recalls quietly, "Let us remember: Our mother and father survived Hitler's Final Solution. It was a miracle. No one could possibly comprehend what they went through."

POLAND: EARLY 20TH CENTURY

Our story begins in the early 20th century with two children who are born in Poland. Little did they, or their families, know about events that were closing in around them. Events that would lead to the Final Solution enacted under the orders of neighbor Germany's Chancellor, Adolf Hitler.

The Tishgarten family of Pinczow and the Goldbergs of Kalisz.

THE BEGINNING

In 1917, Felix Goldberg was born in a small town outside of Kalisz, Poland. Bluma Tishgarten, was born nine years later, in 1926, 190 miles away, in the town of Pinczow.

Both children were born into happy, growing families. Felix had four siblings as did Bluma. They grew up as typical Jewish children secure in the love of their mother and father. They went to school, played games with friends and did chores for their parents. Bluma loved to ski with her family in the winter. In the summer, she swam in the lake near her home. Felix played soccer and often attended soccer matches with his cousin in the stadium in Kalisz

Felix and siblings
at Cheder

Both families continued their long-standing traditions observing the Jewish Sabbath (sundown Friday–sundown Saturday). On Friday night, Bluma's family lit the Sabbath candles and said their weekly prayers. On Saturday mornings, Felix and his siblings attended Synagogue. Most other days, he attended Cheder (the name for school where Jewish children learn the Hebrew language and religious customs). But by the time Felix and Bluma were teenagers, it was clear that things were anything but normal in Poland. Their families were aware of the pogroms of the past — violent riots which drove Jews from towns they had lived in for generations. In many cases, they were killed. Now, Felix and Bluma's world was about to be turned upside down.

Their parents had heard rumors that Jews in other cities and towns were being harassed and treated poorly by Adolf Hitler and members of his Nazi Party. Some reports indicated Jews were being killed, but the Goldbergs and Tishgartens were skeptical. "This couldn't happen to us," they thought.

The Nazis were a German political party that grew into a movement that blamed Jews for many of their problems. The Nazi plan was to eliminate the Jewish way of life — to limit their movements, take away their jobs and destroy anything and everything Jewish — including publications. Books written by Jewish writers had been burned in public displays years earlier.

The burning of books in Nazi Germany on May 10, 1933.

Jews were considered "enemies of the state," and an active propaganda campaign began to convince Germans (and others) that Jews were bad and needed to be controlled. Violence against Jews was widely encouraged and as a result many Jews suffered under the hands of German troops as well as German and Polish citizens.

Slowly the rumors became fact as the war came to Felix and Bluma's hometowns. In September, 1939, under Hitler's orders, the Nazi army invaded Poland. One morning, Felix saw his father removing the family Mezuzah from the front door.

"Why are you doing that?" he asked his father.

His father looked at him, his brow creased with worry. "I've been watching what's happening to our friends and neighbors. It's no longer safe to be identified as Jews. We need to keep a low profile at least for now."

The world was changing quickly for Felix's family. Christian neighbors who had been their life-long friends and neighbors were suddenly angry enemies, telling their children, "You're not allowed to play with Jewish friends."

World War II had officially started. From the air, German planes rained bombs down on homes, theaters, schools and businesses. Thousands of German troops crossed the border and began destroying everything in their path.

When the Nazis arrived in Pinczow, the first thing they did was to burn it to the ground, leaving Bluma and her family homeless. Bluma was just 13 years old and her closest sister, Cela, was 15. The family escaped to an uncle's house on the outskirts of town.

"Daddy, are we safe now?" Bluma asked, meeting her father's worried gaze. "I'm afraid. "

"For now, sweetheart," said her father. "But I don't know about tomorrow. I just know we must be vigilant. We might soon have to move away from here, too, because it's getting increasingly dangerous for all of us to survive."

But the Nazis came looking for them again. They had a mission and would not stop until they destroyed their way of life and killed every Jew they could find.

2

CAPTURED

1939 – 1940

_A_S part of the Nazi effort, signs were erected around Polish cities and towns where Jews existed. These signs read "Jews Forbidden" in areas where their movements were restricted. Other signs read "Do Not Help Jews — To Do So Means Immediate Death."

In English: Jews not wanted here.

Signs and posters were part of a massive propaganda campaign designed to convey the idea that the Jews were the problem and that they must be eliminated.

For the time being, the Tishgartens and their Jewish friends were allowed to remain in town, but their access to school and stores was restricted. They had a curfew and had to be off the streets at 6 p.m. each night. They wore that yellow Jewish star on their clothing so as to be easily identifiable.

BLUMA

Bluma and Cela's parents had carefully considered what the family would do if and when the situation got worse. Her father had already joined the resistance and was now fighting with them.

On a quiet morning as the family prepared for the day, they and their mother heard gunshots. She carefully peered out the window to see Nazis marching neighbors from their homes at gunpoint.

Frightened, she called to Bluma and Cela, "Come here, NOW. I need you to listen to me carefully. The Nazis are here, and they'll kill us if we don't act quickly. Take these." She handed them money and the beautiful pieces of gold jewelry their father had given her over the years. She gazed with sadness at her wedding ring before tucking the money and jewelry into the girls' pockets.

"Momma," said Bluma, confused.

"Listen to me." Her mother's voice was desperate. "It's all I have. It will help you survive. I'll wait for your father. You must GO now! Run out the back door into the woods and hide. Don't come back, no matter what."

"But Momma, what will happen to you and Papa?" pleaded Bluma.

"We'll try to get away, but you must…"

The shouting was getting louder. Someone was heading toward their door.

"Save yourselves for Papa and me. I love you. GO!"

She opened the back door and pushed them through. Cold November air stung Bluma's lungs. She had never known her mother to be so strong or forceful.

Tears were now streaming down her and Cela's faces. Distraught and scared, they ran into the woods until they could no longer see their house. Their neighbors were doing the same, but rather than join them, something told the girls to run the other way.

Cela, a born leader, drew ahead and turned back waving her arm. Hurry, we have to run faster. You can do it, Bluma."

Bluma's lungs burned. But fear and grief burst through her. "Where are we going?" she called to Cela. "Where?"

"I have an idea," said Cela. "We'll hide here in the woods tonight. No one will find us."

It was getting dark. Cela brushed away leaves from the ground under an ancient oak tree. "This will work," she said.

"But," said Bluma.

"No buts," said Cela. The girls settled their backs against the tree, hugging each other to ward off the cold. But the fear deep within their bellies made them shiver.

That was the beginning. For weeks, they stayed at the edge of the forest, sneaking into the towns they passed, trading the jewelry their mother had given them for food, hiding in sheds. When the jewelry was sold, they begged for food. Still, they tried to keep their spirits up even though they were filthy and near exhaustion.

In the woods, Cela and Bluma meet up with a cousin from Pinczow. After a period of time hiding with him and others from their hometown, the weather grew colder. They knew they would have to leave the forest.

They hid during the day, and walked at night for several days until they arrived in the town of Chmielnick. They hoped to stay with an uncle there. While hiding outside his house, they realized the Germans had been told about them.

One day, Cela, who had been so brave, turned to Bluma, her eyes glazed and defeated. "I'm tired of all this running and hiding is bound to get us caught and perhaps killed," she said.

"What do you think we should do?" said Bluma.

Later that day, an answer came. From a distance they heard a voice booming over a loudspeaker. "Jews, give yourselves up now and you will not be harmed. We will take care of you. Come into town tomorrow."

"I don't trust them," said Cela, "but we can't keep running. Now might be the time to surrender. Do you agree?"

"I don't know," said Bluma. "I'm not sure." She paused and studied Cela's hopeful face. "But as long as I'm with you, I'll feel safe."

The next day, with their hands raised high over their heads, they walked into the town's center.

"Halt!"

Two tall blond men in uniforms approached them speaking in German. The men glared at them and led them to an open truck filled with others who had been hiding in the woods. Everyone looked tired, their clothes caked with dirt.

Cela grabbed Bluma's hand.

"Don't worry," she said. "We'll keep each other safe."

The truck rumbled into town and stopped at the train station. Bluma felt Cela's hand tremble when the truck came to a stop in front of a wooden train car, one of a line of cars, its door open.

"*Raus*, out!" shouted the soldiers, pushing the girls and the other frightened passengers out of the truck and into what the girls saw was a train car that only recently had carried cattle to market. People were already crowded inside, but somehow Bluma, Cela, and twenty more who had been in the truck with them were crammed in, side by side unable to sit.

The door slammed shut. A woman next to Bluma wept. The train began to move.

"I can hardly breathe," said Bluma.

"Me either," said Cela, looking toward the door they had just entered. "Try to move closer to the door," she whispered, nudging Bluma past the woman next to them. "There's a gap. Perhaps we can move to that small opening near the door. Can you breathe now?"

"Not very well," said Bluma.

"At least we can huddle together to stay warm," said Cela, and the girls wrapped their arms around each other.

FELIX

Nineteen year-old Felix Goldberg wanted to survive as much as Cela and Bluma. He was older and had more options. I'll fight for the Polish army, he thought. They need me. He was assigned to the cavalry and did his best, but his unit was overtaken and captured by Nazi soldiers.

Like all Jews, he was required to wear a six-pointed star, identifying him as Jewish. He decided to take a chance and removed the emblem. He would risk riding the commuter train without it. Soon, with his dark hair and deep brown eyes, he was singled out. "Juden. Jew!" said a soldier who was guarding the train.

The soldier forced him off the train and began hitting him, cracking him across the face with a force so hard it knocked out two of his teeth. "You will go back to the Warsaw ghetto," he shouted. *(NOTE: The Nazis assumed he was a prisoner in Warsaw, but he was not.)*

I don't want to go to the ghetto, thought Felix, glaring at him.

And he didn't. Instead like Bluma and Cela, he was jammed into a cattle car with a hundred others, his back pressed against the door

"Where do you think this train is taking us?" said a man standing next to him.

"I don't know," said Felix, "but I don't plan to stay much longer. This train will certainly take us to our deaths. I want to survive."

Slowly, Felix opened the train door...just enough to get through it and jumped. He hit the ground hard, rolling several times before stopping. I have to get up, he thought. On shaky legs, he stood and ran into the woods.

He wandered for days, his clothes ripped, his body a painful bruise. He was fortunate to make his way to Tulish-kov, the home of his grandparents, where he stayed for almost a year. But fearing getting caught, he decided to leave and the Nazis caught him again, this time sending him to the Auschwitz concentration camp.

He barely remembered lining up for the selection process that sent some men directly to the gas chambers and others like him to the barracks where he was forced to work in rain, mud, ice, snow, his feet raw and chapped with cold. He was awakened at four in the morning and marched in formation out of the barracks where he and his fellow inmates stood in the freezing weather for hours and for no reason. Men fell dead around him.

Still, the Nazis counted each man to make sure no one had escaped. In the distance, he could see smoke rising from a chimney, morning, noon, and night emitting an oily, acrid odor, but neither he nor anyone else, knew why. He was more worried about the gnawing hunger that never left him. He worked so hard and was fed so little, a breakfast of coffee, thin soup with the same meals repeated at lunch and dinner.

Day by day the number of inmates thinned as the weakest among them died of disease and starvation. He had been assigned to the Jawarzno Coal Mine. The workers marched two hours there every morning. Once they arrived, he was in charge of the elevator which brought men into the depths of the earth and back up again. The work was dangerous and often the walls of the mine collapsed, killing whoever got caught in the rubble.

Felix not only sent men into the mines, he also was now bringing up the bodies of those very same men at the end of his shift. He was told to put the bodies, no more than skin clinging to bone, into the back of a truck, which unbeknownst to him, made its way to the crematoria.

Still, Felix knew that if he wanted to live, he had to take risks, so he sometimes stole bread and wine from the guards and hid his treasure in a place he shared with no one.

One night, two years after his capture, upon returning to Auschwitz from the mines, he discovered that a large part of the camp had been targeted and destroyed by the Russians who had bombed the camp by air.

LIBERATION OF MAJOR NAZI CAMPS, 1944–1945

NEUENGAMME
May 1945

WESTERBORK
April 1945

WOEBBELIN
May 1945

SALZWEDEL
April 1945

RAVENSBRUECK
April 1945

BERGEN-BELSEN
April 1945

SACHSENHAUSEN
April 1945

GERMANY

GREATER GERMANY

POLAND

DORA-MITTELBAU
April 1945

BUCHENWALD
April 1945

OHRDRUF
April 1945

GROSS-ROSEN
February 1945

MAJDANEK
July 1944

THERESIENSTADT GHETTO

FLOSSENBUERG
April 1945

GUSEN
May 1945

DACHAU
April 1945

GUNSKIRCHEN
May 1945

MAUTHAUSEN
May 1945

LANDSBERG
April 1945

EBENSEE
May 1945

★ LIBERATED BY THE UNITED STATES

LIBERATED BY GREAT BRITAIN

LIBERATED BY THE SOVIET UNION

AUSTRIA

Map based on source material from *Historical Atlas of the Holocaust*, published by the United States Holocaust Memorial Museum.

As Allied Forces moved in from the west and and the Soviets surged from the east, they were shocked to discover the conditions of Jews and other prisoners in the Nazi concentration camps. The soldiers liberated the camps as they continued to close in on Nazi forces in their drive to Berlin.

3

EVERY DAY
A MIRACLE, JUST
TO SURVIVE

1943 – 1944

BLUMA

Bluma and Cela were now working in a munitions factory making bullets for the Nazi army. They had become slave laborers, starving and tired, but their lives were safe because their work was needed by the Nazis. Somehow, they'd managed to keep their health unlike so many others who had died of typhus, tuberculosis, and dysentery.

They knew to fear the supervisor, a man with dark gray hair who held cruelty on his face. One day while they were making bullets in a munitions factory, Bluma who had been working long hours, splattered the hot metal on her arm. Her skin turned red. Pain shot through her, but she couldn't stop or the supervisor would send her away.

On another day, as she stood at the machine spitting molten lead into molds, she was so very tired, she could hardly keep her eyes open. They grew heavier and heavier until against her will they closed and she nodded off. She felt a sharp slap on her face, saw the fury in the commander's eyes, saw the other girls turning their heads. "Get back to work," he commanded.

She was terrified.

This was the end, but to her surprise, he calmly walked away. From then on, no matter how tired she was, she reminded herself never to close her eyes again.

At night, exhausted, she fell asleep in the barracks…her body pressed against Cela and five other girls who slept in her small space on the wooden bunk. Often, she woke up in the middle of the night and wondered where her parents and her brothers and sisters were. Had they survived? If so, where could they be? When would she see them again? She prayed that day would come.

One bitterly cold night, Bluma had finally fallen into a deep sleep when the door to the barracks crashed open, jarring her and Cela from restless sleep. *"Alle wachen auf; Everybody wake up!"* shouted a Nazi guard. *"Raus! Schnell.* Out! Fast! You have five minutes!"

"What do you think is happening?" Bluma whispered to Cela.

"I don't know, but I have a bad feeling," said Cela.

They dressed quickly. Outside, shivering and scared, they joined women and girls from the neighboring barracks. Soon, they were walking toward the train station. This time the destination was Bergen-Belsen Concentration Camp.

Unlike previous camps, this time they were given showers and prison clothing. They were assigned a bunk with several hundred women, sharing a bed with many others.

After several months at Bergen Belsen, Bluma and Cela found themselves again in cattle car. Cela held Bluma's hand and gathered her courage. "Where are we going?" she asked the guard walking next to them."

He glared at her, hate filling his eyes. "Be quiet," he snarled.

It was as if Bluma was still dreaming. A train waited for them. Its doors opened, a gaping mouth ready to swallow her and Cela in darkness. They jammed into a corner, fear stiffening their bodies. Two hours later, they arrived at another camp and were herded into a new barracks. This one had more women and less blankets, which were filthy and stiff. Bluma looked at Cela knowing that this many people together in such a small space could only lead to disease and death. We have to hang on, she thought.

After breakfast of soup that tasted like warm dirty water and a hard crust of bread, they were led to a clearing in the woods to a makeshift factory surrounded by airplanes.

As the women waited in line for instructions from a supervisor who sat at a desk stacked with papers, Bluma studied the planes. They were small and sleek and she knew they were there to work, but what could she possible do?

When her turn came, the supervisor looked up from his paper. "Do you know how to paint?" he said.

"Yes, of course," she said. If it means I live, she thought, I can learn to do anything.

Days turned into weeks of marching through brutal cold in thin clothes and painful wooden clogs to the woods where she spent days painting Nazi swastikas and numbers on the side of planes. Eventually, it began to take its toll.

Cela, like many in their barracks, had contracted typhus through a bite from the horrible, itchy lice that crawled on their skin. A cough rattled her thin frame. Her fever rose, sending terror through Bluma's heart.

"I fear I won't live much longer," she said, her voice full of pain. "Please, can you get some medicine for me or more food?"

"I will try," promised Bluma. She knew that leaving be barracks at night was a huge risk. What if she got caught? What might happen then? She was sure they would kill her. But for her sister, she would do anything for Cela who had looked out for her throughout their long ordeal together.

She waited until nightfall. The camp had grown quiet, and the guards were in their quarters when she quietly sneaked out of the barracks, avoiding the constant glare of roving searchlights, and into the empty kitchen. Even though it was freezing, her heart pounded, but she didn't feel the cold. In the shadowy darkness, she found an apple and put it into her pocket.

Back outside, she scanned the camp. No one was out on such a bitterly cold night, so she carefully made her way back to the barracks.

When she reached Cela, she tried to smile as she took the apple from her pocket and handed it to her. "Eat slowly," she said softly. "Please try to save some for later."

"God bless you dear sister," said Cela, and took the smallest bite, savoring the sweetness as relief settled over her flushed face.

Later, when Bluma got sick, Cela took care of her, wiping her forehead, saving bits of food. We will help each other survive, they vowed.

FELIX

Each day had become a fight for survival.

One morning, Felix found himself in a long line. He didn't know why, but at the front on the platform stood a Nazi officer who towered over everyone else. He had heard about this man, Dr. Josef Mengele. "Watch out for him," everyone said. "He's dangerous."

Out of a single line of men, Dr. Mengele was dividing them in two. "What's happening?" he asked the man in front of him.

"He's choosing who will live or die," the man said. "Pray you get assigned to the right."

Dr. Mengele was known as the "angel of death." On this, and most days, he decided who was weak or strong. Those judged to be strong were sent off to work. The weak went to their deaths.

It was Felix Goldberg's turn to be examined by Dr. Mengele. I will live, he thought, and straightened his shoulders.

He tried not to show his fear when the doctor asked him to lift his shirt. The doctor was inspecting him like he was a piece of meat, pressing his arms, his biceps.

"You'll do," said the doctor. And pointed Felix to the right.

4

COULD IT GET MUCH WORSE?

JANUARY – FEBRUARY 1945

FELIX

*I*T appeared the Nazis were losing the war. As the Soviets closed in, the Nazis evacuated Auschwitz. Felix was marched into the woods and overland with no destination. He knew that thousands of men like him had already died inside the camp and this march would no doubt only kill more. The weather was brutally cold. The Jewish prisoners had little if any clothes and many had no shoes—just one or two pairs of socks. SS guards would shoot anyone who appeared to tire, slow down or get out of line.

The men marched arm-in-arm. One of Felix's partners was a man named David Miller, who, like him, was determined to survive. They made a pact, when one of them got tired, he would sleep on the other's shoulders as they marched

When one of their fellow inmates died, those nearest to him would quickly take socks or other clothing for themselves.

It's every man for himself, thought Felix.

When they reached a large open potato farm, the guards agreed to let the farmer cook potatoes, taking two for themselves and allowing their Jewish captives one. If a prisoner took two, they would be shot on the spot.

One farmer decided to do what he could for these bedraggled men. He **boiled potatoes** for the marchers as they **moved past** his farm.

The **SS Guards** threatened to **shoot** anyone who **took more** than one.

Felix didn't care. He was starving. He got in the line for his first potato and ate it. Then he got back in the line for another. He was not recognized, but he had already figured that if he was going to die, it would be on a full stomach. It was during this famous death march that Felix and others were put on a train once again for days. Eventually they ended up in Buchenwald.

Felix went through the line at least **six times.**

The Nazis **failed** to notice.

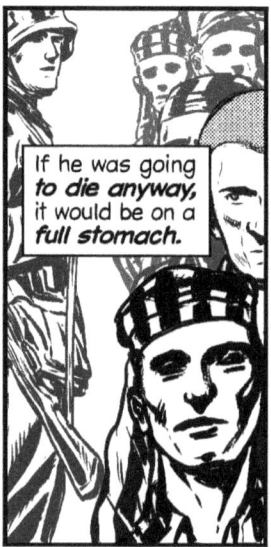

If he was going **to die anyway,** it would be on a **full stomach.**

It just didn't matter **anymore.**

5

LIBERATION

APRIL 1945

FELIX

It was near the end of the war and the prisoners at Buchenwald concentration camp knew it. There were rumors and now signs: they could hear planes and bombs draw closer. Many of the guards had fled their posts.

Felix recognized the signs and decided NOW would be the best time to make his move. And move he did.

He decided the best place to hide was underneath the barracks that had housed him for the past three months. They'll never find me here, he thought. With a few turnips hidden in his pocket, he crawled under the barracks in the dark of night and there he stayed for three days.

Each morning, as the prisoners lined up for roll call, the guards called Felix's name. Two of the prisoners looked at each other. One mouthed, "Where's Felix?" and the other just shrugged his shoulders as if to say "I don't know."

The guards called Felix's name again, but there was only silence. Felix knew this was a risk, but he had taken risks before. The guards searched for him but never under the barracks.

He was cold and starving, the turnips having been eaten. He was losing all hope when a miracle happened. Soldiers were arriving, American and Canadian and British. He could hear their accents, felt the confidence in their steps. Carefully, he came out of hiding to discover that the camp had been liberated. He was free.

Days later, weary, hungry and relieved, he and his fellow survivors met General Dwight Eisenhower, who was touring the liberated camp and who one day would become president of the United States.

April 12, 1945. Dwight D. Eisenhower views the bodies of prisoners at Ohrdruf, part of the Buchenwald concentration camp complex.

The future president was shocked at what he saw. He told his tour guides he wanted to see every "nook and cranny."

After which he wrote: *"I felt it my duty to be in a position from then on to testify at firsthand about these things in case there ever grew up at home the belief or assumption that 'the stories of Nazi brutality were just propaganda.' .... as soon as I returned to Patton's headquarters that evening, I sent communications to both Washington and London, urging the two governments to send instantly to Germany a random group of newspaper editors and representative groups from the national legislatures. I felt that the evidence should be immediately placed before the American and British publics in a fashion that would leave no room for cynical doubt."*

CONGRESSMEN SEE NAZI CAMP HORROR

BUCHENWALD, Germany, April 23.—(AP.)—Eight American Congressmen agreed today, after inspecting the horrors of Buchenwald prison camp that the evidence of Nazi atrocities committed there exceed the wildest flights of imagination.

Representative Carter Manasco (Dem.), of Alabama, after he and his companions had been shown around the camp—where emaciated bodies of the Nazis' victims are still stacked like cordwood, where men were hung on spikes like sides of beef until they died, and where bodies by the hundreds were burned in furnaces, said:

"This is the most horrible thing that anyone could conceive."

Representative Gordon Canfield (Rep.), of New Jersey, declared the evidence bore out everything that had been said or written about Nazi brutality. He said:

"This is barbarism at its worst."

(In Paris it was reported that two French journalists released from the notorious Buchenwald concentration camp estimated today that between 150,000 and 200,000 persons died there.)

The Congressmen who were in Britain on various missions, were invited to come here by Gen. Eisenhower so that they might obtain first-hand evidence of the atrocities committed in Buchenwald. Other members of the group were Henry M. Jackson (Dem.), of Washington; Earl Wilson (Rep.), of Indiana; Albert Rains (Dem.), of Louisiana; Eugene Worley (Dem.), of Texas; Marion T. Bennet (Rep.), of Missouri, and Francis E. Walter (Dem.), of Pennsylvania.

Behind one building the Congressmen saw a great heap of wasted human bodies, which the Nazis had left piled up one atop the other, like so many logs. Nearby was a truck piled high with 60 more bodies, each bearing a tattooed prison number.

In the adjacent courtyard was a pile of ashes and bits of bone—remains of the dead who had been burned in the 12-furnace crematory, where blackened skulls still could be seen.

Below the furnaces the congressmen were shown a room from which the prisoners said none of their number ever had emerged alive. Along the walls were hooks like those in a butcher shop, and prisoners said human bodies—including some that still had life—were hung there until the furnaces were ready.

The Americans took Buchenwald 11 days ago and conditions have improved considerably since then, but there is no way to erase the tragedy as long as any of the 21,000 prisoners whom they released are still present.

An Associated Press story, published on April 23, 1945, four days after Eisenhower's request that journalists come and witness for themselves.

One of the American journalists who visited Buchenwald was Edward R. Murrow, a broadcaster for CBS. Murrow regularly reported on events from Europe to anxious radio listeners at home. On the occasion of entering the concentration camp, Murrow described the scene for his audience: "There surged around me an evil smelling of horrors. Men and boys reached out to touch me. They were in rags and the remnants of uniforms. Death had already marked many of them, but they were smiling with their eyes."

Eisenhower also insisted that Germans from a nearby town visit the camp to see what had been done in their name. In addition, he required American soldiers to tour the camp, so that they could see the evil they were fighting.

BLUMA

Bluma was now nineteen years old. For six years she had been under the watchful eye of Nazis, but no longer. On April 29, an American Army unit entered Kaufering, a subcamp of Dachau that housed mostly women including Bluma and Cela, and liberated it.

Weak and sickly, Bluma and Cela were overcome with joy when an American soldier reassured them that everything from now on would be "alright." Years later, Bluma would wish she had asked for the soldier's name. She thought of him so often and wanted to thank him for comforting her.

She and Cela were moved to a hospital with warm blankets, fresh water, and flavorful hot broth staffed by kindly nuns. Slowly, they were nursed back to health.

Little did Bluma know that liberation would bring her and Felix together for a bright future.

When she and Cela were healthy enough to begin their new lives, they were sent to a Displaced Persons camp. There was no barbed wire or guards. There were clean streets and apartments, places to socialize, dance, see movies and theater.

The camp was paradise, but as they recovered, Bluma and Cela tried to find their parents and siblings. Bad news followed bad news. In their hearts, they knew their parents hadn't survived. Still, they held the thinnest ray of hope because the truth was too painful to say aloud.

Bluma had put on some weight and was feeling better, so she decided to have her picture taken. She was introduced to Felix Goldberg, the photographer. A spark flew. He's handsome, she thought.

Felix, on the other hand, thought, I can't wait to take a picture of this pretty young lady. He took his time, using light and shadow to capture what he saw in her, curiosity and kindness and smarts.

Bluma liked Felix. He had a sense of humor and a confidence that she knew was part of his character. When he delivered the photograph to Bluma, she asked if she could pay him.

"Yes," he said, his eyes twinkling, "with a kiss."

She blushed and refused. He kissed her anyway. Thus began their lifelong romance.

Life moved fast after all they'd been through and Felix and Bluma were eager to grab every moment. Soon they married and as they waited for their application to emigrate to America to be approved, they also waited for the birth of their first son, Henry.

Cela had also married and left for the United States where she and her husband had settled in South Carolina. All immigrants needed a sponsor to support them until they got on their feet. Since immigrants needed a sponsor in order to be resettled, the Hebrew Immigrant Aid Society (HIAS) along with the Jewish Federations of North America and Columbia's Beth Shalom Synagogue were instrumental in this important move.

Finally, Felix and Bluma's applications were approved and the day came to leave their past behind. They boarded a transport ship that brought them from Germany to New Orleans. And a train brought them to Columbia, South Carolina.

They arrived with a bit of change in their pockets, no English, and their young son. Life in America was going to be an adjustment.

But the community welcomed them with open arms. Much work had been in place before their arrival. Committees were formed to help the new residents find jobs, learn English, find a home and get new clothes.

6

A NEW LIFE

1949

*F*ELIX began work as a janitor, and eventually started his own business, selling ceramic tile. Today, the Tile Center is still thriving.

Bluma later joined him in the business. They had two more children, a boy, Karl and a girl, Esther. Life was good.

Eventually as their children got older, Felix and Bluma began sharing stories about their pasts. As time went on, they spoke to school groups who were studying about the Holocaust.

"I know that they're hearing it every year.
But you still have to remind people."

– FELIX GOLDBERG

"In a way, we fear that maybe that's why
we survived—so we can tell the story."

– BLUMA TISHGARTEN GOLDBERG

AFTERWORD

*N*OW that you've read Felix and Bluma's story, it's clear that they did whatever they needed in order to see the next day. They took risks—and miraculously—they survived. At the same time, each of them lost their parents, grandparents, and brothers and sisters. Lives taken by Adolf Hitler and the Nazi Regime's Final Solution.

Thanks to the trust that the Goldberg family put in me, I am here to tell their story. But this journey really started with Felix Goldberg's words. After testifying about his life during the Holocaust experiences, he stepped off the stage at our Synagogue, handed me his speech and said, "Frankie, do something with *this*."

This, resulted in a website for educators and this book.

MY CLOSING MESSAGE TO YOU

Now is not a time to remain silent. Silence is complicity. When you see or hear wrongdoing like bullying or name-calling, call it out. Stand up for what is right. Be an UPSTANDER not a BYSTANDER.

– Frank W. Baker
Columbia, South Carolina

ABOUT THE AUTHOR

*F*RANK W. Baker has worked in television news, public education and public television. In 1998 he founded the Media Literacy Clearinghouse website and began work helping teachers and students better understand how to think critically about the media.

Frank has been a frequent presenter at schools, districts and conferences across the United States. His work in media literacy education was recognized by the National PTA and the National Cable TV Association with a national "Leaders in Learning" award in 2007. He also conducted media literacy training with educators in Singapore, Mumbai (India) and Nairobi (Kenya). In 2019, Frank was recognized by UNESCO with its GAPMIL (Global Alliance Partnership for Media & Information Literacy) honor.

He has been published in *Learning & Leading With Technology* (ISTE), *Education Week*, *Cable in The Classroom*, *Telemedium*, *Florida English Journal*, *Ohio Media Spectrum*, *Middle Ground: The Magazine of Middle Level Education*, *Library Media Connection* (LMC), and *Screen Education* (Australia). His first book, *Coming Distractions: Questioning*

Movies, was published by Capstone Press. His second book, *Political Campaigns & Political Advertising: A Media Literacy Guide* was published by Greenwood Press. His third book, *Media Literacy in The K-12 Classroom* was published by ISTE (2012). In 2017, Routledge published Baker's *Close Reading the Media: Literacy Lessons and Activities for Every Month of the Year*.

Baker is also the lead writer on the highly-acclaimed *We Survived the Holcaust: The Bluma and Felix Goldberg Story* graphic novel from Tree of Life Books. The book was lauded by *Publishers Weekly*, calling it a "powerfully moving nonfiction graphic novel." Additionally, *Kirkus Reviews* weighed in with "moving and important." *We Survived the Holocaust* was named to the American Library Association's YALSA 2024 Great Graphic Novels for Teens list and was also a Silver Finalist for Pop Culture Classroom's 2023 Excellence in Graphic Literature Award. The book was additionally a Finalist in the 2024 Jewish Comics Experience (JEWCE) Awards in both the Autobiographical and Biographical Content and Historic Narrative categories.

Learn more about Frank at www.frankwbaker.com.

RESOURCES

PAGE IV-V: Both Felix and Bluma's quotes come from videotaped interviews produced by South Carolina ETV, August 8, 1991.

PAGE VI: Quote by Annie Reneau – https://www.upworthy.com/auschwitz-nazi-camp-holocaust-virtual-tour

PAGE 7: Nazi Book Burning – https://www.washington.edu/news/2007/01/04/fighting-the-fires-of-hate-odegaard-library-hosts-exhibit-on-nazi-book-burnings/

PAGE 11: Jews Not Wanted Here – https://ukrainianjewishencounter.org/en/did-jews-help-the-nazis/

PAGE 19: Map of Concentration Camps, *Historical Atlas of the Holocaust* published by the United States Holocaust Memorial Museum

PAGE 32: General Dwight Eisenhower visits Buchenwald Concentration Camp – https://www.eisenhowerlibrary.gov/research/photographs/world-war-ii-holocaust-images

PAGE 25: General Eisenhower's reaction to what he saw at Buchenwald Concentration Camp – https://newspapers.ushmm.org/events/eisenhower-asks-congress-and-press-to-witness-nazi-horrors

PAGE 34: You can listen to the entire Edward R. Murrow broadcast here: https://collections.ushmm.org/search/catalog/irn1002172

L E A R N   M O R E

VISIT THE STORIES OF SURVIVAL WEBSITE

*Scan the QR code above with your phone camera for more information
about the Bluma and Felix Goldberg and their miraculous story
of risk, resilience, and renewal.*

www.storiesofsurvival.org

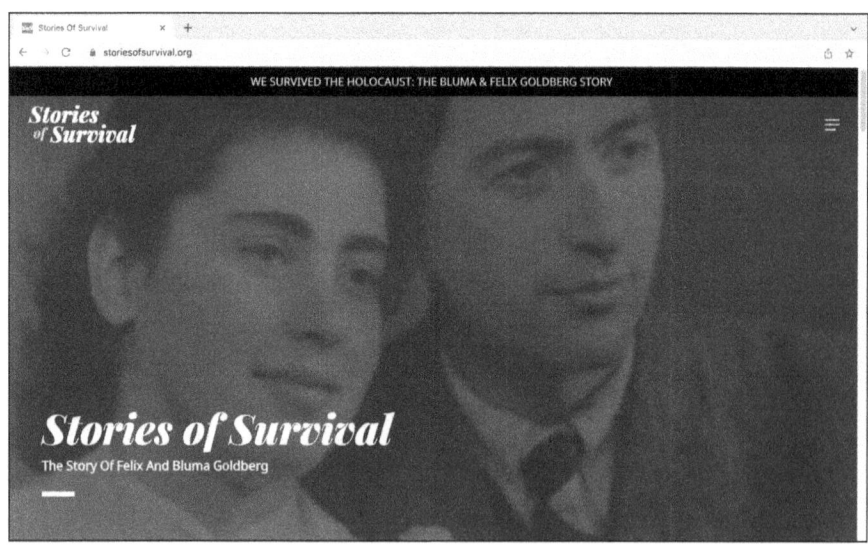

www.ingramcontent.com/pod-product-compliance
Lightning Source LLC
Chambersburg PA
CBHW051558120626
46551CB00013B/1566